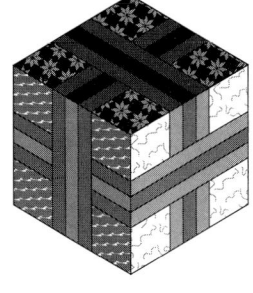

Cubic Ribbons

by Marilyn Doheny

All Rights Reserved   Copyright ©1991 Doheny Publications

Art direction, Graphic Design
and Illustrations: C. Eng Design

Photography: Mark Frey

YARDAGE INFORMATION
RIBBONS AND BOXES

The fascinating illusion of ribbons weaving between box surfaces is created effortlessly with simple, clever, strata sewing procedures. As "gift packages," they also make a wonderful quilt for celebrating special occasions—birthdays, weddings and all parties!

The options for fabric choice are numerous with this pattern because it is really several patterns in one! The ribbon area can be composed of **three ribbons** or **five ribbons**; the box itself can *disappear or appear three dimensionally!* All of these choices can be made incorporating a very select number of fabrics, or can be made from a scrappy collection incorporating numerous fabrics.

To make the proper choices from all of the options, view each of the illustrations and review the photographed quilts featured in this book. After selecting the box style you prefer, it is easy to identify the appropriate yardage information from the **Yardage Chart** below.

Be sure to compare the box fabric(s) against the corresponding ribbons to be sure that all ribbons can be seen against the box fabric(s) selected.

YARDAGE CHART

RIBBONS Select 3 or 5	FABRICS Select Controlled or Scrappy		BOXES Select Invisible or 3-D	BACKGROUND
Three Ribbons	**Controlled** Select 9 fabrics, 3 per value (lt, med, dk): 1/4 yd ea Cut 3 strips each: 1½" x 45"	**Scrappy** Select 27 fabrics, 9 per value (lt, med, dk): 1/8 yd ea Cut 1 strip each: 1½" x 45"	**Invisible** Select 1 fabric: 3¾ yd **3-Dimensional** Select 3 similar valued fabrics: 1/3 yd each*	included 3 yards
Five Ribbons	**Controlled** Select 15 fabrics, 5 per value (lt, med, dk): 1/3 yd ea Cut 5 strips each: 1½" x 45"	**Scrappy** Select 45 fabrics, 15 per value (lt, med, dk): 1/8 yd ea Cut 1 strip each: 1½" x 45"	**Invisible** Select 1 fabric: 3½ yd **3-Dimensional** Select 3 similar valued fabrics: 1/4 yd each*	included 3 yards

* When three different background fabrics are selected, keep them slightly different in value from each other but not *radically different*.

IMPORTANT NOTE: 1. All of the yardage information listed will create *six* cubic boxes.   2. All of the boxes are the *same size*: 18" x 21". If 12 boxes are desired, then the yardage information will have to be doubled. It will be necessary to double the sewing volume for all strata quantities indicated as well.

Acknowledgments: I want to thank every talented quilter/friend who worked with me in the 12 Month Series and submitted their quilts for photographic consideration in this book. It was a delight as well as a difficulty to narrow the field from all of the wonderful choices. A special congratulations to the three generous quilters whose work was selected to feature the Cubic Ribbons pattern variations—take a bow!

From the traditional favorite *Baby Blocks*, comes a spectacular new look for the 1990's! Cubic Ribbons is an entirely new and refreshing pattern structure from a series of new quilt designs by Marilyn Doheny. This entire new series, **Strata Art Quilts–*For Contemporary Eyes Only*,** is available from Doheny Publications.

All of the designs are stunning to view and yet can be easily created from quick sewing and simple Rotary Magic©1989 (template-free) cutting techniques.

Each pattern in the series has a companion product of unique graph paper specially designed for pre-planning spectacular interlocking effects in advance. See ordering information for all books and graph paper in the back of this book. We are pleased to bring you these fascinating new patterns and hope you enjoy creating them.

BASIC BOXES

Be sure to follow the specific information for the box style you are creating.
Two different blocks are identified in the following text: Block A uses a three strip strata unit to create the ribbon area and Block B uses a five strip strata unit to create the ribbons. The specific information provided will create both block styles.

Block A and Block B are the same overall size when finished. They could be used in the same quilt for a unique design. It is important to note that if both box styles are used together, the seams of each will not merge perfectly from box to box (see below). The ribbon and box areas of each style, constitute different portions of the box surface. Height of one box is 21″ and the width is 18″ (left).

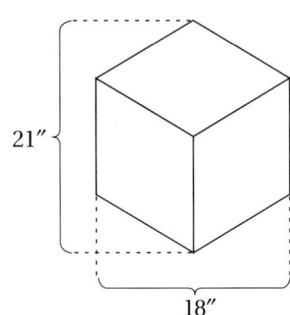

CUTTING THE FABRIC STRIPS

All cutting is very simple, involving only straight lines to create strips. The most *accurate and speedy* approach to quick straight line cutting can be done with **rotary cutting equipment**. The trio of tools is: a rotary cutter, a self-healing mat surface to cut on, and a ruler that is accurate and has visible sight lines with *double,* intersecting 60° angles.

There are many competitive brands on the market. I personally recommend investing in the highest quality products on the market for durability and accuracy to support all of my quilting efforts.

Olfa Products® are the best brand for the rotary cutter and mats. I suggest:
  a) the large cutter, and
  b) the medium mat (or the large one if finances allow!)

Omnigrid™ are the best rulers to have, in fact the only rulers with "double angled" 60° lines which are essential to this project. The most useful and versatile sizes are:
a) the 6" x 24" for all long strip cutting from 45" wide cloth, and the
b) 3" x 18" for ease and maneuverability when counter-cutting the strata units.

It is essential to have at least one of these tools if not both, in order to have double (left and right) 60° angles. If your local stores do not carry these products, we would be happy to send them to you. See ordering information at the back of this book.

A. THREE RIBBON BOXES

There are 27 strips needed for the ribbons: nine strips each of light, medium, and dark fabrics.

Controlled Ribbons: The 27 strips could come from a very controlled fabric selection of only nine fabrics: three fabrics per value, light medium and dark. After selecting nine fabrics, cut three strips of each fabric, 1½" x 45". This will produce 27 strips.

Scrappy Ribbons: The 27 strips could be a very scrappy assortment of 27 different fabrics. Select nine *different* fabrics per value. Cut one strip of each, 1½" x 45". This will produce 27 strips.

Fun Note: (see below)

B. FIVE RIBBON BOXES

There are 45 strips needed for the ribbons: 15 strips each of light, medium, and dark fabrics.

Controlled Ribbons: The 45 strips could come from a very controlled fabric selection of only 5 fabrics per value for a total of 15 fabrics. This would require cutting 15 strips of each fabric for a total of 45 strips.

Scrappy Ribbons: The 45 strips could be very scrappy assortment of 45 different fabrics, 15 per value for a total of 45 different fabrics, one strip for each fabric.

> **Fun Note:** If you make some of the ribbons with *box fabric*, another illusion is created— ribbons spaced apart (**Quilt C**, inside cover).

Figure 1

DISAPPEARING BOXES AND FLOATING RIBBONS (Figure 1)

One background fabric is selected and used for all of the box surfaces. The background fabric must "show off" all of the ribbon strips but not compete with them.

Cut six identical strips:
a) 3½" x 45" for a **three ribbon** box
b) 2½" x 45" for a **five ribbon** box

3-D BOXES WITH RIBBONS (Figure 2)

If a three-dimensional box is desired, then three different background fabrics must be selected. **Cut two strips of each fabric:**
a) 3½" x 45" for a three ribbon box
b) 2½" x 45" for a five ribbon box

Figure 2

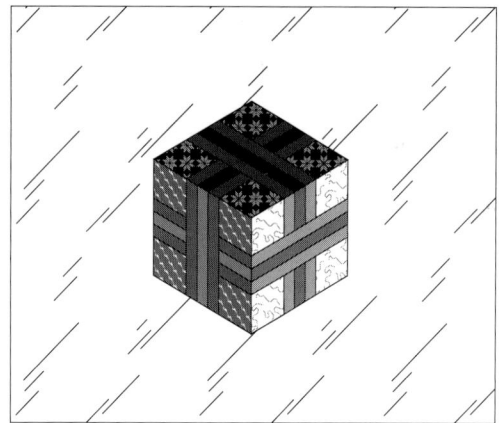 

SEWING THE RIBBONS

All strata sewing for the ribbon area of the pattern is done without staggering the strips. Simply sew them together with a 90° beginning end. The irregular lengths of 45" cloth go to the opposite end of the strata unit (Figure 3).

Figure 3

Three Ribbon

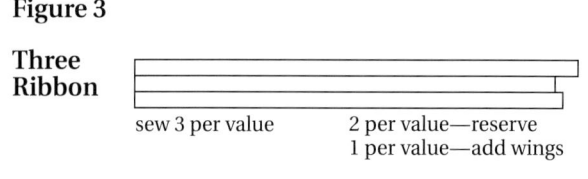

sew 3 per value   2 per value—reserve
                   1 per value—add wings

Five Ribbon

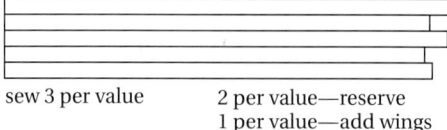

sew 3 per value   2 per value—reserve
                   1 per value—add wings

When sewing strata units, it is important:

1. Not to pull on the strips. This will stretch them irregularly and cause sewn distortions called "lettuce leaves" and "rainbows" (see **CHECK AND CORRECT**).

2. To iron the seams only *after* all of the seams have been sewn and the strata strips are joined which makes them more secure.

IRONING

All ironing must be done *across* the strata seams, *not along* them.

NOTE: Heat and steam are necessary but be careful what you do with them—they are not casual or neutral influences. Over-ironing will distort the strata strips.

1. Iron from the backside first; iron with steam so that the seam allowances go in one direction and lie smooth and flat.
2. Gently pull the strata unit apart as you iron across the short width of the strata seams. Do not iron along the seams, the fabric strips are vulnerable and will stretch in that direction.
3. Turn the strata unit over to the front side and iron again, across the seams while pulling gently apart to eliminate all "accordion pleating."

CHECK AND CORRECT

It is possible that the strata units that you have created are not perfect. But this does not mean that they are not useful! It simply means that they need a bit of extra help. It is important to eliminate distortions as soon as they appear. The trick is in learning what the distortions are, how to correct each of them, and how to get back on track with the quilt construction.

First of all, you want to check that you have even, consistent widths of *each* fabric strip running the entire length of the strata unit. You also want to have an overall "straight" strata unit. Many things can contribute to the distortions during each of the cutting and sewing sequences.

1. If you have seam work that is causing irregular widths, now is the time to correct it before proceeding with any counter-cutting. They can be attributable to: a) poor cutting consistency, b) poor ironing, or c) improperly taken seam allowances.

a) If the distortion is due to poor ironing, then re-iron the strata to remedy "accordion pleating." Grasp the width of the strata and pull it apart to check for popping. If needed, re-iron and proceed on. The strata should be as tall, flat and wide as possible.

b) If the problem is due to poor cutting consistency, unfortunately nothing can be changed at this point. The cuts are real—they are done. Replace the strip(s) with correctly cut strips.

c) If the distortion is due to improperly taken seam allowances, then simply redo the seam from the backside. This can either be done by taking the seam allowance larger, or by removing it and taking less of an allowance. Be sure to re-iron before counter cutting.

2. You may have strata distortions that look like lettuce leaf edges or like a small rainbow arch. These can be "worked around." As you work through the counter-cutting sequences, you will continually cut away any distortion while constantly maintaining a 60° angle at the strata end.

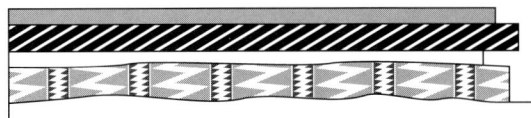

Narrow/Wide Channel Distortion
Adjust seams to be consistent before counter-cutting.

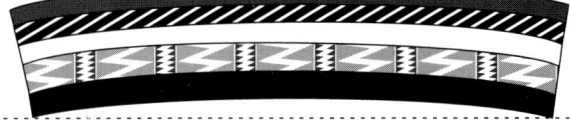

"Rainbow" Distortion
It will be necessary to maintain the 60° angle after each diamond is cut. Trim off the strata distortion before cutting the next diamond.

DEFINITION: Accordion pleating is a crease that has been established during ironing by not exposing the strata to its full sewn height. Aggressive ironing (across the seams) is necessary—it causes the strata unit to attain its full sewn height. If all accordion pleating is not eliminated, it will cause an inaccurate strata height resulting in several counter-cutting errors which make counter-sewing more difficult and the block accuracy suffers.

ADDING THE BACKGROUND WINGS

All of the strata units look similar at this stage. From this point on, there will be two distinctly different strata units. They are referred to as the "over ribbons" and the "under ribbons."

1. For all box styles, select three strata units, one per value, to become the *under ribbon* area of each box surface. These units require some additional sewing.

a) Wider strips of fabric which create the box area of the pattern, are added to each edge.

b) The strips of box fabric are referred to as the "wings" on the ribbons, or *ribbon/wing strata*.

2. The remaining strata units become the *over ribbons*.

3. Take the strata units selected for the "under ribbons" and add the background wings to each of them. **All wings (background fabrics) are added to the strata units using a specified stagger.**

ADDING THE WINGS

1. a) the three ribbon box gets 3½" x 45" wings.
   b) the five ribbon box gets 2½" x 45" wings.
2. The wings are sewn onto the top and bottom edges of the strata unit. Be sure that you use the correct wings for the correct ribbons.

   a) If three different box fabrics are being used, be sure that the wing fabric is being added to the appropriate ribbon unit, i.e., light wings go with light ribbons, medium wings go with medium ribbons and so on.

   b) If all of the background is common for a floating illusion, then all six wing strips are the same fabric.

3. **Be sure to stagger the wings as indicated in the diagrams.** After each wing is added, the entire strata unit should stagger downward and to the right.

   a) The three ribbon box has a 2" offset (Figure 4A).
   b) The five ribbon box has a 2½" offset (Figure 4B).

Fig 4A Three Ribbon — offset wings by 2"

Fig. 4B Five Ribbon — offset wings by 2½"

COUNTER-CUTTING LOGIC FOR ACCURACY

For strata, it is essential to use an internal seam as the guide for establishing any angle. Do not use a fabric at the edge of a strata unit—all internal distortions are reflected at the edges of a strata. It is not a "true" point from which to guide counter-cuts. A strata unit is analogous to a lake where every seam, like a water skier or swimmer, can potentially cause a rippling disturbance. These distortions accumulate at the edge of the strata as they do along the shore of a lake. The "calmest" area of both is the center.

RIBBONS WITH WINGS (*Under Ribbons*):

Before counter-cutting any of these *ribbon/wing* strata units, measure the full "height" of the strata unit. Make a written note of that measurement. You will use this exact measurement to establish the counter-cut width for the "ribbon only" (*over ribbon*) strata units. The measurement should be approximately 9½".

THREE AND FIVE RIBBON VERSIONS:

1. Measure the height and make a written note of it (Figure 5).
2. Establish a 60° beginning angle (Figure 6).

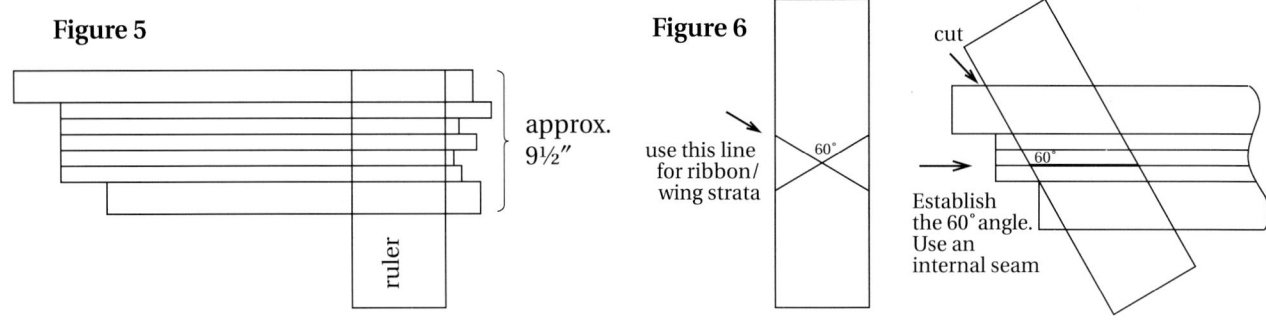

Figure 7A

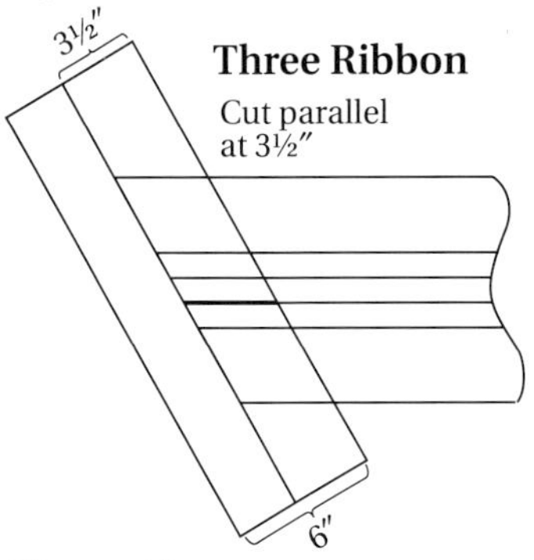

Three Ribbon
Cut parallel at 3½"

Figure 7B

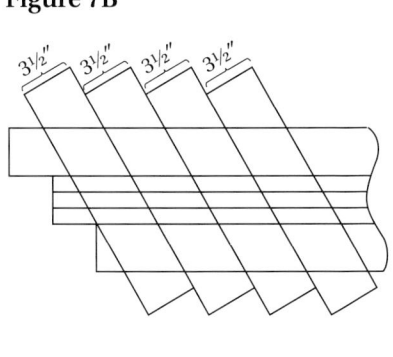

Figure 8A

Five Ribbon
Cut parallel at 2½"

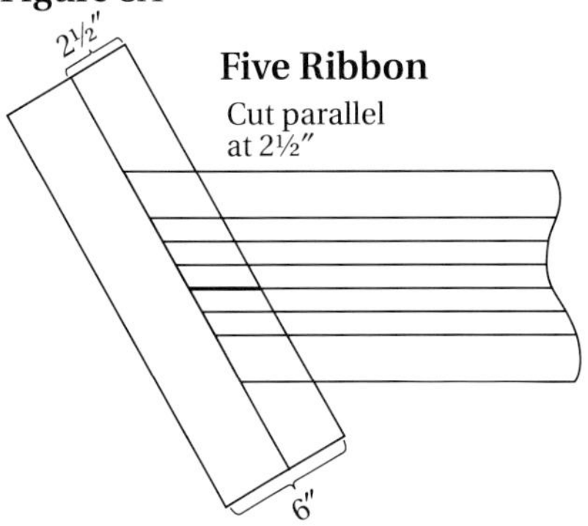

Figure 8B

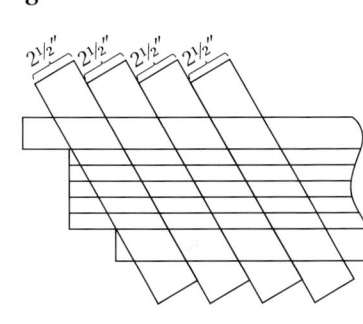

3. a) Counter-cut the three ribbon strata unit at 3½" wide (Figs. 7A and 7B). Use the *exact angle* and the 3½" measurement specifically as shown. It *must be parallel* to the 60° angle and 3½" wide.

b) Counter-cut the **five ribbon strata unit** 2½" wide. Use the *exact angle* and the 2½" measurement specifically as shown (Figs. 8A and 8B). It *must be parallel* to the 60° angle and 2½" wide.

4. Be sure to check and maintain the 60° angle often. Do not assume that it is correct!

5. Clean up any irregular edges from lettuce leaves or rainbow distortions as you go (Figure 9)

Figure 9

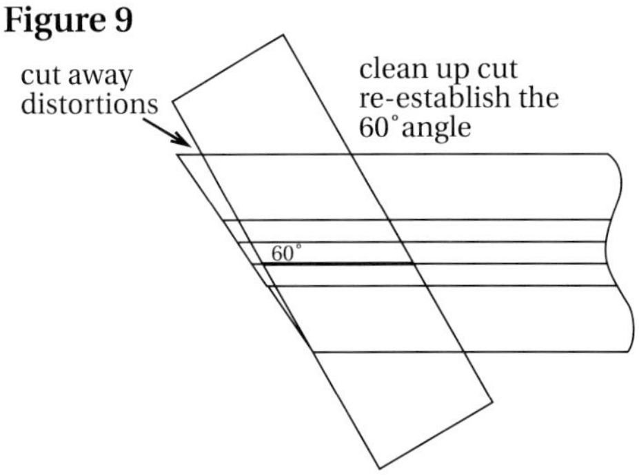

cut away distortions
clean up cut re-establish the 60° angle

OVER RIBBONS:

1. Establish a beginning 60° angle (Figure 10). **Be sure to use the exact angle indicated in the illustration. This is the opposite 60° angle.**

2. Use the e*xact* measurement of the height of the "ribbon/wing" strata unit for the width of this counter-cut. This measurement should be about 9½". **It will be necessary to use two rulers "side by side" to get the proper width** (Figure 11).

3. Be sure to check and maintain the 60° angle often. Don't assume that is is correct.

4. Clean-up any irregular edges from lettuce leaves or rainbow distortions as you go.

5. Continue to counter-cut the ribbon only strata units into approximately 9½" parallel lengths. Use your own appropriate measurement (Figs. 12A and 12B).

Figure 10

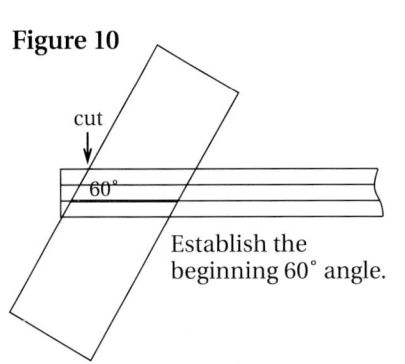

cut
60°
Establish the beginning 60° angle.

Figure 11

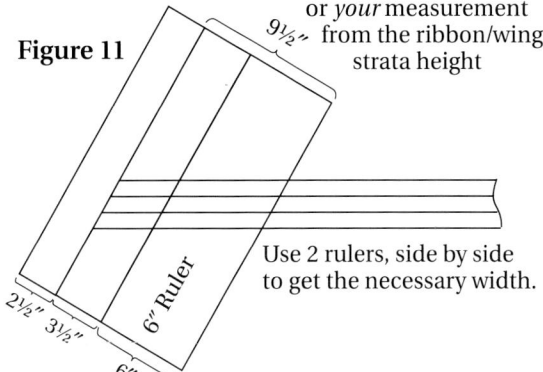

or *your* measurement from the ribbon/wing strata height

Use 2 rulers, side by side to get the necessary width.

Figure 12A

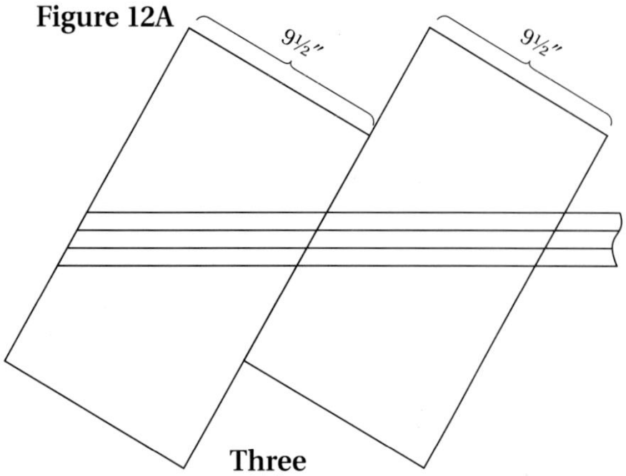

Three Ribbon

Figure 12B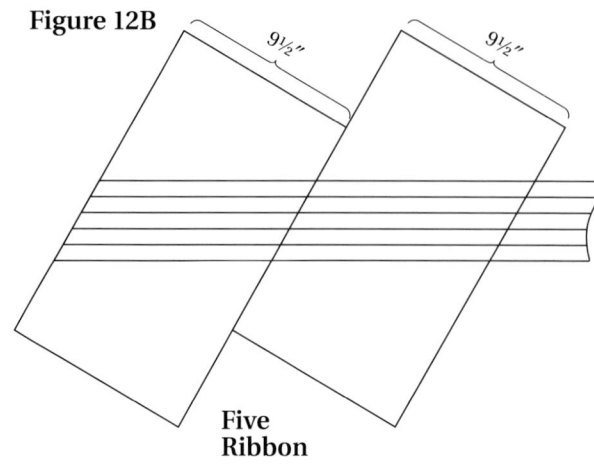

Five Ribbon

CREATING THE BOX SURFACES INDIVIDUALLY

This is the easiest sewing of all—there are no seams to match! However, there are opposing angles to "offset" (Figure 13).

IMPORTANT NOTE: It is important to use "opposing angle" seam work when aligning the wings onto the ribbon unit to take the 1/4″ seam to join them. Use Figure 14 to show proper alignment.

a) The two edges of cloth must be aligned to cross each other 1/4″ inward from the edge at both ends, top and bottom.

b) The seam must be *start and exit exactly* where the crossing occurs, i.e., where the seam starts and where the seam exits.

Figure 13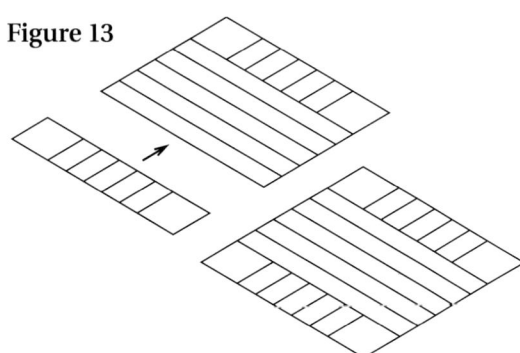

CHECKPOINT:

If the seam was taken as it should have been; exactly at the crossing of the two edges, then the union of the two should have produced a straight line at the external edge. There should not be a stair-step upward or downward at the seam area from one part to the next (Fig. 15). Check and adjust as necessary. *The edges of the diamonds must have straight lines in order to sew straight seams when joining them to create the boxes.*

Figure 14

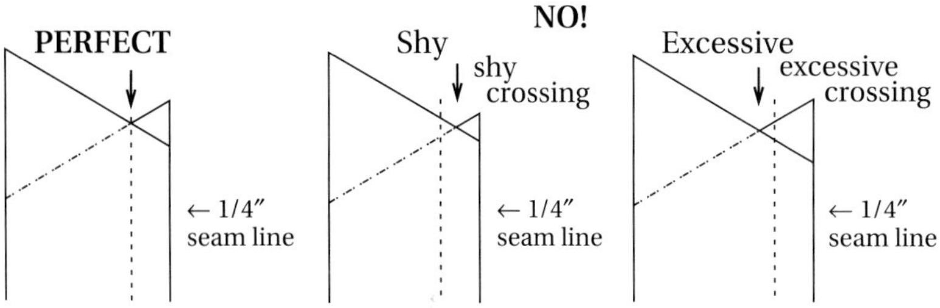

PERFECT — Shy / shy crossing — **NO!** Excessive / excessive crossing
← 1/4″ seam line   ← 1/4″ seam line   ← 1/4″ seam line

1. Select two wings and one ribbon, per value.

2. Sew them into a unit. The light wings always sew onto a light ribbon, medium to medium and dark to dark.

3. There should be at least six diamonds created per value.

4. These six diamonds will combine to create six cubic boxes.

Figure 15 problem areas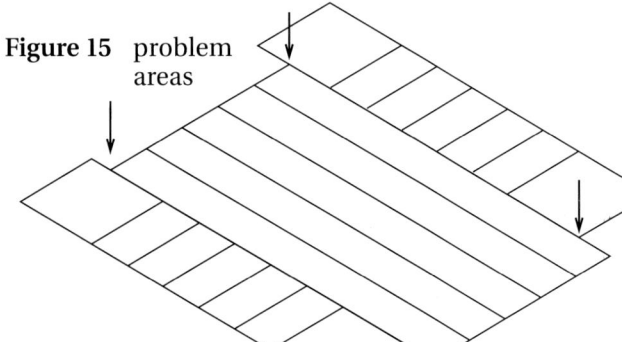

GENERIC BLOCK CONSTRUCTION

For both styles, six cubic boxes need to be created. Each will have one light, one medium, and one dark diamond sewn together.

PLANNING THE LIGHT SOURCE

Figure 16

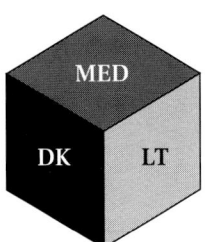

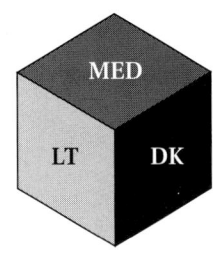

There are choices to be made concerning the arrangement of values within the box.
1. Before sewing the boxes together, arrange two different combinations of the light, medium and dark interplay as shown (Figure 16).
2. Walk around the arrangement viewing each value as the "up" surface—this "changes the direction" of the visual light source (Figure 17).

Figure 17

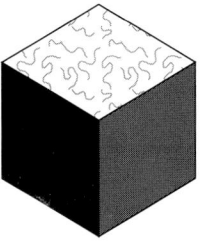 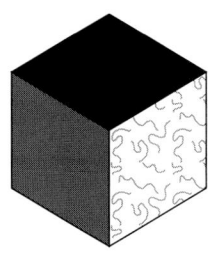

Sunrise   High Noon   Sunset

3. Select the one that appeals to you after viewing your blocks. Let your blocks talk to you! Don't go by what you like in the diagrams or photographs, let your work have a say. *Your fabrics will work together in an individual way.*
4. All of the blocks will sew together in this arrangement. This means that whichever light-medium-dark arrangement is selected, all blocks will have the same arrangement.
5. The blocks can feature any one of the values as "up" in the final quilt set.

> NOTE: Having all of the blocks with the same arrangement of values, and having the quilt feature the same organization of the blocks based upon value, is called *maintaining the light source*. Since this entire effect of three dimensional ribbons is really an illusion, it is critical to help the illusion by maintaining the light source.

PREPARING THE FIRST SEAM

Figure 18

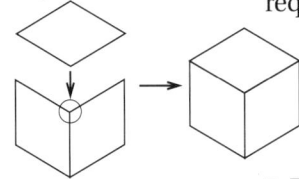

Sewing three different diamond surfaces together requires inset piecing. The circled areas represent the "inset" area of one block (Figure 18). When sewing seams which require inset seams:
   1. Leave the last 1/4" of the seam (at the inset area) unsewn.
   2. Back stitch for strength.
   3. Iron the entire seam in one direction.
   4. Then re-iron the last 2" of seam allowance (at the inset area) open.
5. Turn the unit over and begin to "inset" the next part by sewing from the backside so that all intricate seam areas are exposed where the inset is taking place.
NOTE: Be sure to match strata seams along the edges of each diamond unit as necessary when sewing the large diamonds together. They should nestle easily. Change the direction of the seam allowances with your finger tips as necessary to redistribute the thickness and to help the seam junctions match more easily.

THE INSET SEAM

Always position the two units together exposing the underside of the project so that you can *see* the seam allowance of the inset area.
   1. Line up both fabric shapes so that they match exactly to start the seam (Figure 19).
   2. Leave any necessary unsewn 1/4" beginning seam areas for future inset sewing.
   3. Begin the stitch from the outside edge and stitch toward the inset or pivot area (dead

Figure 19

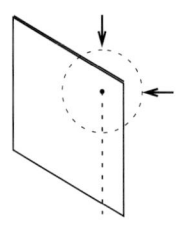

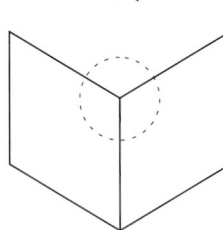

center of the opened seam allowance). The seam allowances should all be in full view (Figure 20).

4. *Have the needle in the fabric*, dead center of the seam which is ironed open.

5. The needle should be in the cloth just between each seam allowance. If the previous seam (see arrow) is correct, the needle has stopped exactly at the point where *seam A* stopped and is back stitched (Figure 21).

Figure 20

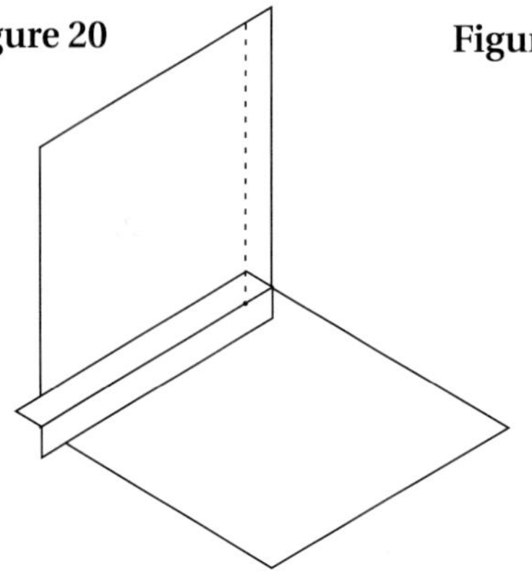

Figure 21

needle

seam A

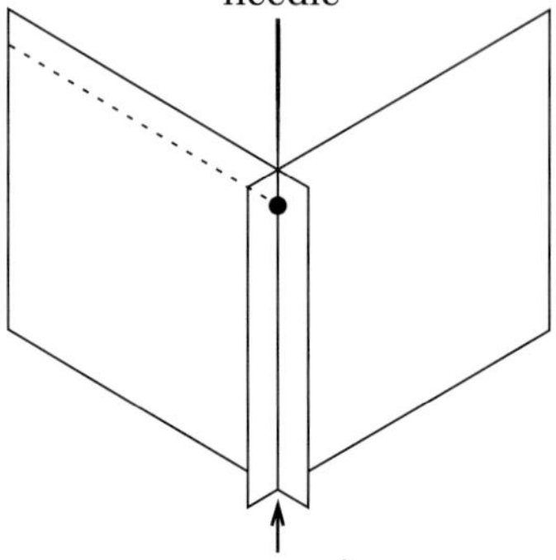

THE PIVOT SEAM ACTION

1. At the inset or pivot area you will lift the pressure foot and rotate the entire unit of cloth together in a counter-clockwise (not clockwise) motion. ***Rotate all fabrics together.***

2. Turn them counter clockwise until the piece being "set in" is travelling directly from the needle towards your chest. This is the "under" piece of cloth (Figure 22).

Figure 22

needle

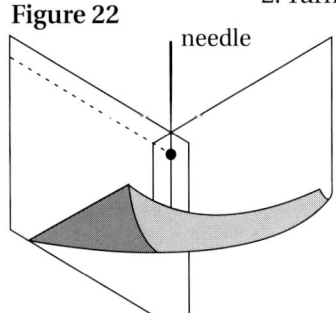

NOTE: It may be necessary to roll up the "above" fabric unit to expose the "under" fabric. This will line up the edge of the lower unit of cloth from the needle towards your chest.

3. Using your right hand, hold the "under" piece of cloth in this position on the throat plate of the sewing machine.

4. With your left hand begin to rotate the top unit to the left and back of the needle area. To do this:

a) maintain a "pull forward," and

b) rotate clockwise action, "to the left and back." You may need to repeat this process several times if the "above" unit is large or long.

5. Stop the rotation action when the exit edge of the above unit and the edge of the (under) "set-in" piece line up parallel. Whichever way they line up, heading from the needle to your chest, keep both edges parallel for the entire exit seam (Figure 23).

Figure 23

needle

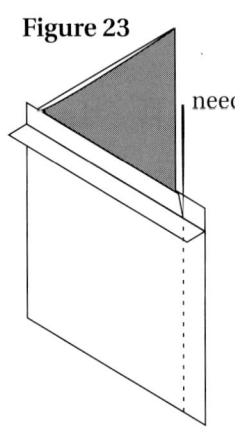

6. Drop the pressure foot and:
   a) sew out to the exit edge, or
   b) sew to the next pivot (inset) area.

7. Repeat the Inset/Pivot Procedure.

Figure 24

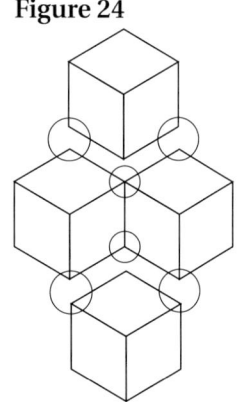

NOTE: If you are insetting *one row* of boxes into another, there will be numerous and continuous insets and every other inset/pivot will not be convenient, i.e., having the inset seam area underneath and hard to see.

8. Rows of inset boxes have numerous insets internally and also at the edges for insetting the background cloth (see circled areas Figure 24).

THE BACKGROUND CLOTH

It is possible to applique the boxes onto a background cloth, or to cut strips of background cloth and inset them—a choice must be made.

It is easy to create the background cloth shapes if you rather sew than applique.
1. Layout one diamond surface and make a parallel measurement—use the full measurement including seam allowances. This will determine its parallel wall size (Fig. 25).
2. Cut large strips to this size.
3. Establish a 60° angle. Be sure to cut the proper 60° angle you need, A or B (Figure 26).
4. Inset the strips around the perimeter of the box edges.
5. As you go, join the seams between the background pieces.
6. Trim the external edge to the desired final size and shape (Figure 27).

Figure 25

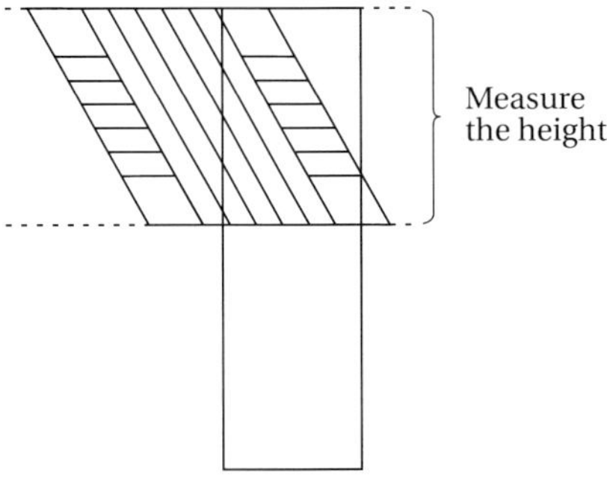

Figure 26

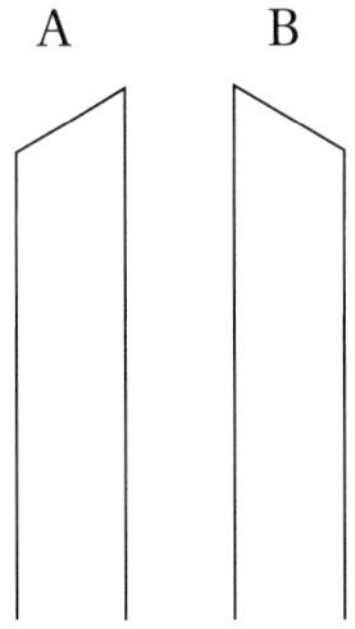

Figure 27

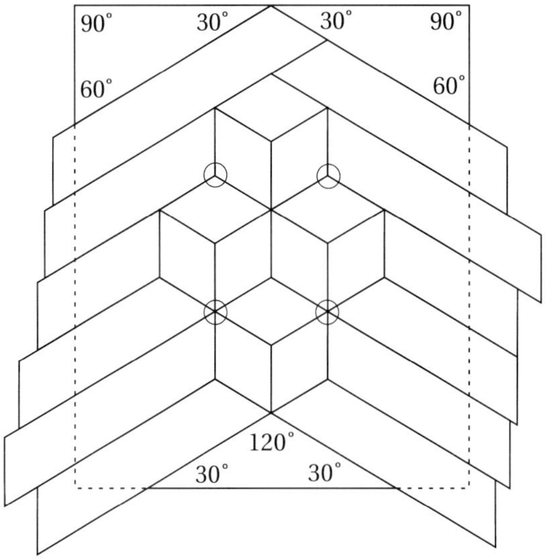

BACKGROUND FABRIC BEYOND THE BOXES!

You can use the information in this book to create additional box styles and sizes with unique (irregular) ribbon areas. The ribbons can be an assortment of widths (Figure 28)—anything goes!

The rules:
1. The cut-size of the fabric strip for the background wings is also the counter-cut size of the ribbon/wing strata unit.
2. The height of the ribbon/wing strata unit is the counter-cut width of the ribbon only strata.

Use the illustrations for inspiration, they are guidelines and tips to help you invent your own boxes. Have fun and enjoy your surprise packages!

Figure 28

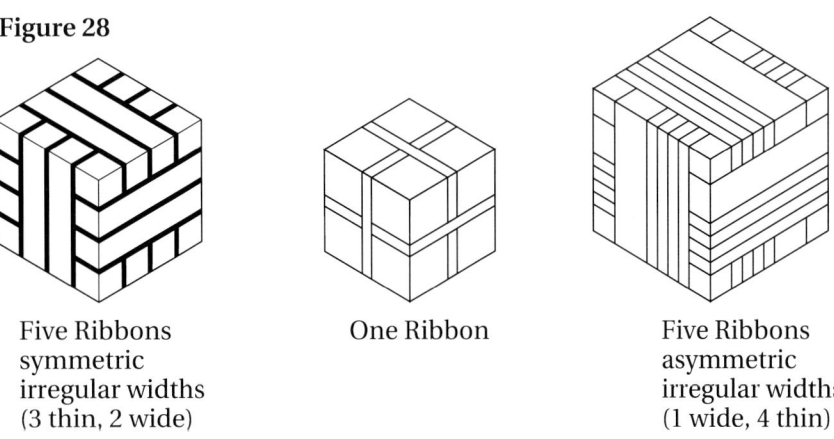

Five Ribbons symmetric irregular widths (3 thin, 2 wide)

One Ribbon

Five Ribbons asymmetric irregular widths (1 wide, 4 thin)

About the Author

Marilyn has always been both a people person and a fabric person. She started making quilts in 1982. The first of her three children was then nine months old, and she desperately needed an outlet with lots of adult interaction. So, to save her sanity and work with fabric, she enrolled in a six-week basic quilting course. During the entire six weeks, each student attempted to piece one pinwheel potholder using a single triangle template, then quilt it, and bind it. Truly, great things come from humble beginnings. Marilyn never finished that potholder (although it does hang, "in progress," on her sewing room wall). She was hooked and began to search the public libraries for books of quilt patterns. She then discovered that there are shapes other than triangles and was suddenly and overwhelmingly in love with the endless possibilities!

Since then, Marilyn's life has included every aspect of quiltmaking, from creating her own quilts to teaching others about the art. With joy and enthusiasm she has made hundreds of quilt tops and has inspired and instructed others to do the same. Marilyn is always dreaming up new patterns and inventing innovative sewing techniques for the traditional favorites. Her quilter's world is full of artistic achievements that "piece together" and give purpose to the joys of her life: color, texture, fabric, geometric patterns and people.

Other quality products from **Cutting Edge Quilt Designs**™ and **Doheny Publications**.
Available at your local quilt store, or write to us at: P.O. Box 25151, Seattle, WA 98125

45° Kaleidoscope Wedge Ruler $16.96
Create clever, magical Kaleidoscope illusions fast and easily with this superb tool! Includes complete instructions with quick quilt pattern.

9° Circle Wedge Ruler $18.95
Infinite circular designs! Innovative new ruler includes instructions for 20 different patterns. Create spectacular quilts or clothing embellishments.

■ PATTERN BOOKLETS
featuring Marilyn Doheny's Rotary Magic© techniques for perfect cutting without templates

Amish Sparkle Star $6.95
A delightful interpretation of a traditional Amish pieced pattern.

Maple Leaves $6.95
Falling leaves is the motif of this wonderfully soothing quilt. Use up to 175 different fabrics for these 25 leaves — a great scrap quilt opportunity!

Trailing Vines $6.95
A glorious scrap quilt inspired by Susan McCord's antique quilt (1846), in the collection of the Henry Ford Museum. For hand or machine applique. Sections of the design can be used for clothing embellishments as well.

■ OTHER PATTERN BOOKLETS
Canadian Geese $7.95
Stunning, award-winning 52" quilt featuring two majestic Canadian Geese. Complete paper patch applique instructions.

Reticule $7.95
Original design of a "country lady's purse" used by women in the early 19th century to transport needle work projects. You will be delighted with its charming appearance as well as its remarkable usefulness. Quick and easy to sew. Includes instructions for three sizes.

Feathered Wishbone $4.95
Six versatile fine hand quilting motifs for blocks and borders.

■ BOOKS
And if you enjoyed this book, other new titles from the **Strata Art Series**—*For Contemporary Eyes Only!* are:
Cubic Pinwheels $10.95
Cubic Ribbons $10.95
Triad Interlock $10.95
Woven Ribbons $10.95

Goosey Hearts $14.95
A lavishly illustrated 64-page book of original applique and hand quilting patterns featuring a full size fold-out of the Goosey Hearts quilt (38" x 28").

■ DESIGN ACCESSORIES
Kaleidoscope Design Grid $4.95
Graph paper featuring 4 and 6 division wedges for use with the 45° Kaleidoscope Ruler.

9° Circle Design Grid $4.95
The perfect accessory for designing elaborate spiral motion patterns for the 9° Circle Wedge Ruler.

Graph paper for the *Strata Art Series*
Triad Interlock Design Grid $4.95
Cubic Pinwheels Design Grid $4.95
Cubic Ribbons Design Grid $4.95
Woven Ribbons Design Grid $4.95

■ ROTARY CUTTING EQUIPMENT
Omnigrid™ **Ruler** 3" x 18" $8.95
6" x 24" $12.95
Olfa® Rotary Cutter (large) $15.95
Replacement blades (bulk 10) $36.00
Cutting Mat medium $21.50
large $39.00

Please send orders to:
Cutting Edge Quilt Designs™
P.O. Box 25151
Seattle, WA 98125

Include $1.50 shipping and handling for paper products;
$2.50 for rulers and cutting mats

Wholesale inquiries welcome.
Prices subject to change without notice.